DESCENDING DOVE

Author
Melanie Woolner

Cover artwork and illustrations
Rebekha Burton

Illustrator: Rebekha Burton

RWG Publishing
PO Box 596
Litchfield, IL 62056
https://rwgpublishing.com/

Published in the United States of America

Paperback: 978-1-68411-794-9

It is by the grace of our Father, lord of heaven and hell, ruler of the earthly plains, that this book has been written and illustrated through two sisters in Christ with hearts of love, honour and obedience.

As you read the words given by the Holy Spirit and take in the artwork, we pray that you will be blessed.

For almost a year we have been persecuted by the enemy and have come through the darkness and into the light, through great personal cost we have been down in the valley, but now are on the mountain top. Such is the power, might and glory of God.

Thank you Jesus for all you do for us, your servants forever
Amen.

Dedicated to
God the Father, Christ the Son and the Holy Spirit.
Amen

Acknowledgements

Melanie's poems are straight from the heart and express real life in a way that the reader can identify with on a deep level. I particularly related to "How can I trust a man" in my own life. The spirit of the Lord speaks through the poems and connects with the heart to bring healing, conviction and love to the believer and non believer alike. The imagery portrayed through this beautiful poetry is almost tangible. The words express explicitly the nature and character of God the Father, God the Son and God the Holy Spirit.
Praise the Lord. *Zoe, sister in Christ.*

These poems are straight from the heart of God.
Melanie has declared herself a servant of God and by doing so is a witness to his glory. These poems are for anytime of life, but particularly for certain times when the Holy Spirit reveals their depth of meaning.
David and Arlene Cadman
Bible study leaders
Church of the Nazarene
Morley, Leeds, England.

I've known Melanie for 5 years and truly believe that our God has knitted our souls together in a beautiful Philia love of tight friendship. Her poetry comes directly from God while walking with him in the early hours every morning. Its from one of these walks that she contacted me and declared that the spirit told her that I was to work on the illustrations for this book. "As soon as I saw your first sketch I knew it had to be you! Your depth of meaning, beautiful symbols and Gods given talent shone through." ~ *Melanie: Feb 17th 2019*
I am greatly blessed with her as a friend and mentor.
Rebekha Burton: Artist, illustrator, friend, child of Christ

Table of Contents

Foreword

Descending Dove is straight from the heart of God. I feel overwhelmed and truly blessed to Know that the words given to me are so personal, so special and so meaningful.

I truly hope that the reader can identify with these words on a personal level.

The Spirit of the Lord spoke to me through these poems
and hopefully does to you too, which, in turn, gives you love and healing
where and when you need it.

The beautiful art work is just as I imagined and from the beginning, I knew that Rebekha was in tune with the Holy Spirit, her work making the book whole is truly inspiring and no one else could have done that.

Thank you, Lord

Written by Melanie Woolner's hand using the words of the Holy Spirit.

The Abyss

I reach for you with outstretched arm,
I grasp and claw and cry out loud,
I go into the pit, the belly of the beast,
Not for me a table and feast,
But biting and rasping and scratching at least.

The darkness is stifling, no air in here,
I slip down the well and into the fire,
Aching, breaking, yawning mire.

A wasted life, oh, why didn't I listen!
The few who spoke God's words in my ear,
But much too late now I fear.

Salted with fire and peppered with regret,
For all the hours spent with beer and debt,
With nought to show but being tossed around in the sea and fret.
I can't bear the sound of the heavenly choir,
As I slip down and down the wire,
Into the abyss of nothingness, unrequited love has nothing on this!
But I fear that's what this really is,
For it's not my spouse, my friends I miss,
But God of course! How I could kiss the sweetness of his heavenly lips,
But not now, now I'm in the pit!
A wasted life of a fool like this,
Am I to spend eternity in this abyss?
I cannot bear; I will not have it,
I will claw and scrape my way out of it!
But to no avail, alas I had my chance and I blew it!
So now I cry, I snivel, I wail.

The dragons breath draws ever near, I fear,
I fear, all is lost, my dear,
Please don't live your life like me,
I regret all my days spent drunk and wild and fancy free,
I leave this world with nothing gleaned,
But my debts and all the pain I see,
 In those drawn around
That were foolish enough to love me.

AMEN.
By The Holy Spirit using the hand of Melanie Woolner.

The Blanket of the pit

I felt so alone,
Surrounded by people,
I started to cut myself off,
I shied away from all around,
The pit of despair was my home,
My comfort, my all that abounds.

As I sank deeper into the blanket,
The deep, deep blanket of the pit,
I grew tired, heavy, weighed down,
Nothing lifted me up,
Nothing was good in the world,
All I could see was darkness,
And all I could feel was cold.

Then, out of the dark,
A hand reached out,
A hand so strong,
It pierced the gloom,
It pulled me out of the pit of despair,
I was rescued from the doom.

I found myself in tears,
Wailing, crying,
Begging to be set free,
From all the darkness in the world,
From the darkness living in me.
The hand that pulled me from the pit,
Touched my very heart,
I started to see the beauty and wonder,
In God's world of warmth, love and light.

AMEN.
By The Holy Spirit using the hand of Melanie Woolner.

Trust

How can I trust a man?
Even a man from the Bible?
He's still a man,
And a man is still a man.

How can I believe what he says?
When all I've ever heard is lies?
All I've ever known is hurt,
Being broken, grieving, messed up or worse.

How can I let someone in again?
How can I ever trust again?
How can I ever believe in anyone again?
I don't think I can.

I've been told to open the door,
Let Jesus in, say the sinner's prayer,
All will be forgiven and my life will start again,
I don't know if I can.

How can I let Jesus in?
How can I trust in Him?
How can I believe in Him?
Can I?

I went to church with a friend,
I felt like a fraud, an imposter,
I was amongst believers, but I wasn't one,
I just wanted to scream and run, could I?

How can I go back to church?
How can I face those people?
How can I let them in?
I can't, can I?

What's wrong with me?
Why can't I be like them?
Why can't I receive Jesus?
Why can't I?

I was encouraged to read the Bible,
I was encouraged to pray,
I was encouraged to attend the church,
I can do this day by day.

I'm now surrounded by people who love,
They love me for who I am,
As broken, lost and lonely as I am,
They are showing me the right path to step on.

I need these people by my side,
I know that I can trust them,
The next step is trusting Jesus,
Who knows where I'll go then?

AMEN.
By The Holy Spirit using the hand of Melanie Woolner.

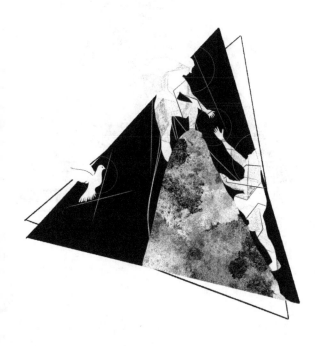

The man in the boat

I had a vision of a man in a boat,
A man in a boat on my front lawn,
A boat nowhere near the sea,
What could this mean to me?

The man was stood, hand outstretched,
Beckoning me forward,
I took a tentative step near,
Then stopped, gripped with fear.

Men that I had known before,
The hurt, the heartbreak, the damage they caused,
I couldn't put myself through that again,
I looked away and tried to block out the pain.

The man in the boat smiled at me,
He seemed to know the mess inside,
He seemed to know about the unhealed scars,
He seemed to know these were my bars.

I was locked in a prison of hurt and pain,
He smiled at me, His hand still reaching,
And in his hand I saw a key,
A key, held out to heal me.

I stepped a little closer,
I dared to trust in Him,
I reached out to touch Him,
And He took me in.

AMEN.
By The Holy Spirit using the hand of Melanie Woolner.

Damaged Goods

Born into an imperfect world,
A helpless babe,
Into the hands of mankind,
She was gently laid.

A perfect blank canvas,
Moulded by love,
Sent into the world,
From Heaven above.

The world was not kind,
The world was not as it is above,
She found she was lacking,
God's glorious love.

Mankind had been given a precious gift,
But all they could see was bad,
All they could see was a burden,
they couldn't see what they really had.

Mankind messed up the holy within,
The child that grew was only on loan,
She belonged to God,
She was going back home.

The world was not her home,
She knew that all along,
The things she experienced,
She knew were all wrong.

When things got out of hand,
When life got really tough,
She called out to Jesus,
He answered her with love.

Jesus had been waiting,
He knew that she would call,
He answered all her questions,
He healed her all in all.

She knew she had come home,
She knew the worst was past,
Jesus was here and would never leave,
He was within and that was cast.

She was maturing,
Growing fast,
Learning of the word,
God was teaching her at last.
She learned a lot,
She quickly grew,
What she had was good,
What she had was new.

She learned God's plan,
She knew her path,
She knew her purpose,
She knew it would last.

She listened to God,
She read the word,
She followed the spirit,
From God she heard.

This life was good,
This life was holy
,Her spirit was flying,
She was no longer worldly.

The world had no hold,
Her spirit was released,
She was a Christian,
Born again in Jesus, totally free.

AMEN
By The Holy Spirit using the hand of Melanie Woolner.

Growing faith

I planted a seed, a tiny seed,
I placed it in the soil, the warm soil,
I watered it, nurtured it,
I watched it grow.

The tiny seed grew a shoot, a small shoot,
The shoot grew taller, and taller,
The shoot grew leaves, green leaves,
I watched it grow.

A bud formed, a tiny bud,
A bud that grew, bigger and bigger,
A bud that started to open, open wider,
I watched it grow.

I saw the bud open, into a flower,
I saw the flower open, spread its petals,
I saw the flower's colours, beautiful colours,
I watched it grow.

The flower was lovely, brightly coloured,
The colours were amazing, truly wonderful,
The flower grew bigger and bigger,
I watched it grow.

A blossom of wonder, a true delight,
A vision of splendour, a remarkable
sight,
A welcome change in the dreary world,
I watched it grow.

From seed to seedling, I watched it grow,
From seedling to stem, I watched it grow,
From stem to flower, I watched it grow,
What will you become, as God watches you grow?

AMEN.
By The Holy Spirit using the hand of Melanie Woolner.

Do you see?

Do you see me?
I'm not sure that you do.
You don't see the real me,
Not like He does.

Do you see my anger?
I think you do.
But you don't see me,
Not like He does.

Do you see my sorrow?
I think you do.
But you don't see me,
Not like He does.

Do you see my pain?
I think you do.
But you don't see me,
Not like He does.

Do you see my hunger?
Do you see my thirst?
I don't think you do,
Not like He does.

Do you see my faith?
Do you see God's face in mine?
I really hope that you do,
For that's what he sees in everything I do.

AMEN.
By The Holy Spirit using the hand of Melanie Woolner.

Do you believe?

Do you believe in Jesus?
I don't know if you do?
I believe He's here, in all that I do.

I don't know if you love him?
But I know that I do,
I believe He's here, in all that I do.

Do you believe in Heaven?
I don't know if you do?
But I believe I'm going,
One day soon.

I don't know if you know this?
But I know that I do,
I believe in Heaven, in all that I do.

AMEN.
By The Holy Spirit using the hand of Melanie Woolner.

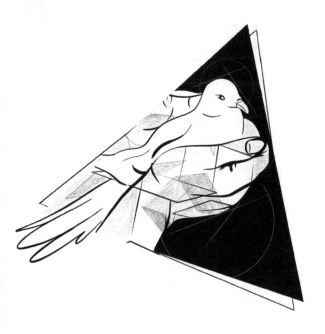

God is good

God is good, yes He is kind,
God is love, He isn't blind,
He sees our worries, He sees our fears,
He sees everything through our tears.

God is good, yes He is grace,
God is mercy, He doesn't haste,
God is love, He isn't blind,
He sees our fight, He sees our might.

God is good, yes He is kind,
God is love, He isn't blind,
He sees our hurt, He sees our pain,
He sees everything that we can gain.

God is good, yes He is just,
God is love, He is a must,
We need Him in our daily lives,
He sees all, He is so wise.

God is good, yes He is there,
God is love, He gives care,
Reach out to Him, hold His hand,
He sees everything that we don't understand.

AMEN.
By The Holy Spirit using the hand of Melanie Woolner.

I was

I was a sinner, now I'm free,
Lord Jesus, you rescued me.
I was in bondage, now I'm set free,
Lord Jesus, you rescued me.
I am delivered, I am set free,
Lord Jesus, you rescued me.
I wait for heaven. For I am free,
Lord Jesus, you rescued me.
You came down from heaven to set me free,
Oh Lord Jesus, you rescued me.

AMEN.
By The Holy Spirit using the hand of Melanie Woolner.

I will follow

Lead and I will follow,
Everywhere you go,
Ask and I will give to you,
All that I know.

Everything I am is yours,
No matter what you do,
For I am in you, Lord,
And you are in me too.

Fix this mess you see here,
Turn my life around,
Make the mess a message,
To help the lost be found.

AMEN.
By The Holy Spirit using the hand of Melanie Woolner.

Why should I?

Why should I worry?
You guide my life,
You use my hands,
You use my feet,
You use my all to show how great you are.

Why should I get angry?
You guide my life,
You use my thoughts,
You use my words,
You use my all to show how great you are.

Why should I be sad?
You guide my life,
You use my emotions,
You use my belief,
You use my all to show how great you are.

Why should I be negative?
You guide my life,
You use my flesh,
You use my spirit,
You use my all to show how great you are.

AMEN.
By The Holy Spirit using the hand of Melanie Woolner.

Can you

Can you bend and not break?
Can you work and not faint?
Can you be pushed and not snap?
Can you be humble when the proud crack?
Anything is possible for a believer...

Can you be prodded and poked but not react?
Can you be fired up but not get burned?
Can you be calm when all around are flapping?
Can you be peaceful when chaos abounds?
Anything is possible for a believer...

Can you be quiet when all around shout?
Can you be still when everyone else is rushing about?
Can you be listening when all about talk?
Can you stand when the world says walk?
Anything is possible for a believer in Christ.

AMEN.
By The Holy Spirit using the hand of Melanie Woolner.

Salt

Jesus said we are the salt of the earth,
We need to be born again, have a new birth,
A sprinkling of salt to flavour the way,
To help us speak to all today,
To walk the right path,
To live as we ought,
To sprinkle the salt we were given, not bought.

If we are the salt, we need to spread it abroad,
When winter bites, snow and ice blanket the road,
We slip and slide until the salt is down,
Then we can walk steadily, true and proud.

If we are the salt, when weeds pop up,
Shake all over them to keep them down,
Don't let them back in when you think they've gone,
Or they will choke the goodness that lies within.

Get the salt that is God given,
Shake it, sprinkle it,
Spread it around, flavour the sauce,
The goodness abounds,
But don't let the ice, the snow and the weeds,
Get into your life, don't let them breed,
Cover them with salt and you will see,
The blessings of God in your life grow free.

AMEN.
By The Holy Spirit using the hand
of Melanie Woolner.

What is church

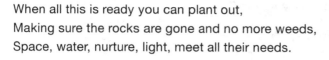

Church is like a packet of seeds,
You don't tear open the pack,
Throw out the seeds and never look back.

You prepare the ground,
You dig up the soil,
Ready to take new life from the toil.

Then you rake the soil,
Settle it down,
Mark where they will sit and grow.

When all this is ready you can plant out,
Making sure the rocks are gone and no more weeds,
Space, water, nurture, light, meet all their needs.

Finally you can watch them grow,
But not sit back and rest, oh no!
They need you to be there and care.

They need your attention constantly,
In case of weeds that sprout up in between,
Choking them and stopping them becoming what they should be.

They need to be watched as insects could eat them,
Animals could destroy them,
They could be forever lost again.

It's not easy watching them grow into maturity,
Making sure they don't stilt or stall,
Stop or fall.

The bad will come, as it always does,
Trying to spoil what God made good,

AMEN.
By The Holy Spirit using the hand of Melanie Woolner.

The jewel

I saw a glint, a gleam of light,
It shone; it sparkled, like a jewel,
The sunlight sparked a star shaped ray,
A piece of treasure discarded, just lay.

I looked closer and caught my breath,
What could be so beautiful and thrown away?
Or was it lost?
A search must be underway?
For something so precious and rare?

As I got nearer, a smile spread across my face,
For what I was seeing was no jewel,
No lost or hidden treasure here,
But a simple raindrop in all its glory.

A small but beautiful rainbow enclosed,
Drop of God's handiwork,
A handcrafted work of art on a miniature scale,
Left for us to enjoy it's beauty, to behold,
If we can take the time, to see God in the small,
In the everyday.

AMEN.
By The Holy Spirit using the hand of
Melanie Woolner.

View through my window

The autumn colours on the trees,
Gold, orange, brown, red,
Matching the colours of the Goldfinches,
As they chatter, squabble, fly overhead.

The squirrel, bounding along the fence,
Bushy tailed, bright eyed and cautious,
Grabbing the monkey nuts in delicate paws,
To hide them until winter bites and food is scarce.

The magpie's cries, brash and coarse,
Scolding, flapping its iridescent wings,
Hidden amongst the black and white uniform,
Swaggering, then flying away to wreak havoc elsewhere.

The beauty that abounds, just from my window,
Staggering, wonderful, and amazing to see,
That God in His infinite wisdom,
Would make all this for my eyes to see.

Such a small snapshot of creation,
But breathtaking for me,
I wonder what else he has in store,
For these wide open eyes to see.

AMEN.
By The Holy Spirit using the hand
of Melanie Woolner.

Praise the Lord

Praise the Lord, O my soul,
I will praise you forever,
I will sing praise to you as long as I live,
I put all my trust in you,
Not mere men,
For you are true,
You are always right,
You guide my life,
When all around me have disappeared,
You are still there.

My hope is in you and you alone,
You made the earth and the heavens,
The sea, the sky, the land,
You are the faithful one.
You give the hungry food,
The thirsty drink,
The prisoners are set free,
The blind see.

You give us a lift when we are down,
You watch over us,
You protect us,
You keep the wicked from our door,
You reign forever,
Praise The Lord, O my soul,
Praise The Lord.

AMEN.
By The Holy Spirit using the hand of Melanie Woolner.

The three blessings of Sarah

Sarah's candle was always lit,
The fire never went out,
From Friday to Friday her tent was filled with light,
Always warm, always bright.

A divine cloud was attached to her tent,
Only leaving her when she died,
But then to return when Isaac married,
Rebecca inherited the blessing that Sarah tarried.

Sarah's tent was always full of food,
The dough lasted and lasted,
There never was a famine, only feast,
In the tent of Sarah, a loving home to the many and least.

Sarah's tent was blessed with love, light, food, laughter,
Comfort, holiness and the presence of God.
Our homes can too, if we really believe it,
If we cry together, love together, eat together and be close knit.

AMEN.
By The Holy Spirit using the hand of Melanie Woolner.

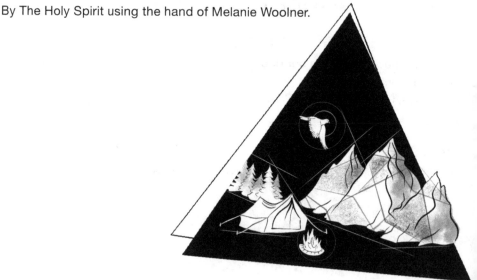

Laughter

Laughter, it makes us smile,
It does us good, for a while,
Sarah laughed when she heard God say,
That she would have a son, in her grey, old days.
But God laughed too, he named the boy Isaac,
Which means "He laughs" so God laughed back.

It's true, laughter is good, and it gives us joy,
It lightens your mood; it's like a new toy,
Even if we pretend, we still have to smile,
But a true laugh is best, even a cackle, a snort, a howl or a whine!

The Bible is full of words of laughter,
Job tells of "mouths full of laughter, tongues of joy",
Paul writes of joy being second to love, the greatest of all the gifts.
But what I like the most is this...
...Proverbs tells us "she is clothed with strength and dignity,
She can laugh at the days to come".
How good is that to know, that whatever happens,
The victory is won?

In the beatitudes, Jesus said "Blessed are you who weep now,
For you shall laugh",
In Philippians we are reminded to "always rejoice in the Lord",
Always be happy in the word, God's sword,
Because He knows how abundantly
He will bless our lives,
If we listen and do what we know is right inside,
So go out, be joyful, sing and dance,
Laugh, smile, jump and prance,
Go with the spirit and you will see
the glory of God when you are set free.

AMEN.
By The Holy Spirit using the hand
of Melanie Woolner.

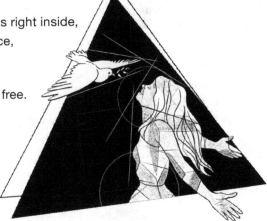

I know

I cry tears of joy,
I cry happiness,
My arms outstretched,
My head held high,
I sob delight at you.
Your pure, holy love that fills me now.

Like a thunderbolt,
Like lightning in my heart,
Your word flows through me like honey.
I know why I'm here!
I know! I know!
You spoke,
I listened,
Your plan is everything I am.

I am a poet,
I can convey your word through my poetry,
You guide my hand,
My life,
My all.
You tell me when to write,
Your love comes through,
Every word, every thought is you.

Thank you, Lord, you overwhelm me,
Your love is in me,
Pouring out of me,
The basics of faith,
Pure love is all around me.
I feel your blessings and they overpower me,
I feel the waves of love as tears fall like rain from the clouds.

I am your waterfall,
A flowing of love,
A heart that is so full,
I feel like I'm about to explode,
Then peace, calm, rest, an aura of comforting love that surrounds me,
Here and now, lifting me up high above the earth and into your arms,
Then back again in waves of love.
AMEN.
By The Holy Spirit using the hand of Melanie Woolner.

Its all you

You painted the clouds into the sky,
You moulded the mountains way up high,
You sculpted the hills, the valleys and rivers,
You shaped the waterways, the land to give us.

You breathed life into us,
You blew your blessings into us,
You shaped us, into who we are,
You gave us life and a life worth living.

You dropped each drop of water onto the seabed,
You placed each grain of sand in the desert,
You pushed each leaf into the trees,
You gave us everything we need.

You mixed the colours to make the rainbow,
You coloured the flowers in the fields,
You made the crops so we could feast,
You made the sun shine down on man and beast.

You made the earth to hang in space,
You shone the stars so bright,
You hung the moon for a nightlight,
You made shooting stars for our delight.

You gave us voice to praise and sing,
You gave us eyes to see all things,
You gave us arms to lift to you,
You gave us feet to go your way,
To walk with you, to follow you always.

AMEN.
By The Holy Spirit using the hand of Melanie Woolner.

Longing

How I long to see your smiling eyes,
Your shining face,
Your mouth that speaks such wisdom,
Your limitless love and grace.

I long to see your outstretched arms,
Your glowing skin,
Your heavenly clothing,
Your crown and then eternity can begin.

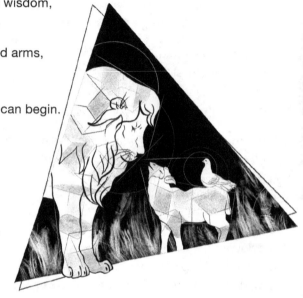

I long to see your hands,
Your feet,
Your side that was pierced,
Your body complete.

I long to see your angel army,
Your orders to fly,
Your strategic commands,
Your mighty battle cry.

I long to see the enemy defeated,
Your victory,
Your overcoming,
Your peace on earth for all to see.

I long to see you in all your glory,
Your power,
Your wisdom,
Your Yes and Amen in your hour, in His story.

AMEN.
By The Holy Spirit using the hand of Melanie Woolner.

A woman like me

How can you use a woman like me?
I pray to you and you speak to me...
Can I weep with those who weep?
Can I retrieve your long lost sheep?
Can I repair a broken heart?
Can I help someone who's had a bad start?
Can I rebuild a broken life?
Can I reconcile a man and wife?
Can I listen and not judge?
Can I be hurt and not bear a grudge?
Can I restore a broken home?
Can I make the lonely not be alone?
No, I can't do any of these things, but the Holy Spirit guides me with wings of love,
Patience, courage and faith, so yes you can use a woman like me and everyone else if we
Can only see, through the eyes of our Lord above, because they are the eyes of love.

AMEN.
By The Holy Spirit using the hand of Melanie Woolner.

A woman of God

She is a roaring lioness,
A fierce warrior,
Her shield is her faith,
Her sword is the word,
She is a woman of God.

She is a fighter in battle,
A soldier in the war,
Her breast plate protects her heart,
Her belt is truth in the Lord,
She is a woman of God.

She is a protector,
A helmet guards her mind,
Her shoes are peace wherever she treads,
Her footsteps walk the narrow path,
She is a woman of God.

She is a battler, a fighter,
A woman, wife, mother,
Her family is protected,
Her home is a temple,
She is a woman of God.

AMEN.
By The Holy Spirit using the hand of Melanie Woolner.

In the cool of the day

You walked with Adam in the cool of the day,
Before the sun arose in the garden.

You walk with me in the early hours of the day,
That is our time to converse in our garden.

You tell me what I need to know,
What I need to grow and to share,
You show me love, affection, teaching and care.

You taught me how to read the word deeper,
To let the spirit guide me,
To help myself and others to learn more about you.

You show me the path, the road I need to take,
To carry on regardless of perils, side tracks or mistakes.

You lead and I follow,
Yesterday, today and tomorrow.
I'm no good on my own,
I stumble, I fall, and I need you in my life,
I can't do this alone.

You are the teacher, the guide, the respected friend,
The Father I thought I would never have or need,
The one constant in a sea of change,
My anchor in the storm of life.

AMEN.
By The Holy Spirit using the hand of
Melanie Woolner.

The secret place

When we love God,
Truly love him,
Give ourselves to him,
Then all things are possible, nothing is impossible,
When we are in The Secret Place.

When we put our trust in God,
There is nothing in between us,
No barriers,
No explaining,
When we are in The Secret Place.

When we spend time alone with Him,
All else fades away,
Nothing else matters,
Nothing is as important,
As our closeness,
When we are in The Secret Place.

When we are together,
In our shared love,
We are as one,
We rest in each other,
When we are in The Secret Place.

A special place,
Only for us,
Only we know how to get there,
A shared secret,
When we are in The Secret Place.

AMEN.
By The Holy Spirit using the hand of Melanie Woolner.

The angels

The room started darkly,
Black all about,
Then a soft light,
Getting brighter all around.

The lights began to sparkle,
To glow brighter,
A glittering, fluttering,
Brightness about.

The colours grew,
The lights were aplenty,
The kaleidoscope shapes,
The colours so strong.

Then a hand touched mine,
I knew it was with love,
The angels touch,
Soft and strong.

The shapes grew together,
They became as one,
The angels sang,
As I sang along.

The waft of wings,
The lights of Heaven,
The Holy singing,
Was overwhelming.

As I lay in my bed,
All this going on around me,
I felt the breeze of the movement,
The angels were watching.

The beating of wings,
The Heavenly choir,
The walking angels,
The Holiness of the night.
I saw their lights,
I saw their shapes,
I felt them moving,
I felt their faith.

AMEN.
By The Holy Spirit using the hand of Melanie Woolner.

The visitation

I was swept upon an angels wing,
Taken to a place of song and sing,
A different path, a spirit place,
I knew not where but oh such peace.

I was taken down a path of light,
The breathtaking wonder of this sight,
A new way of walking, talking, thinking,
Where is this place not of this world?

The pace was swift, the air was still,
The wonder was moving fast as a quill,
But steady, heady, not like me,
A different being at my side.

He spoke of questions, steady from tongue,
I answered slowly, thoughtfully, and true,
He nodded, smiled and said "I knew".
He disappeared as he had appeared,
I knew not from where he came or went,
But he changed me.

Will I ever be the same again?
I hope I'm not!
I want this feeling to last forever,
To be touched by heaven is to be touched by a feather,
A soft, loving, warm, true touch,
But feel it, remember it, treasure it I must.

AMEN.
By The Holy Spirit using the hand of Melanie Woolner.

The vision

I had a vision after praying that my spiritual eyes would be opened,
I wanted to see clearly into heaven,
I asked for guidance from the Holy Spirit,
He showed me what was to come.

The Holy Spirit took me to a busy city centre,
He showed me numbers everywhere,
He told me that the world was full of numbers,
Man's numbers, everywhere.

From birth to death numbers follow us,
They surround us wherever we go,
The number of the beast follows us,
We need not worship it though.

The Spirit showed me people,
Crowds of people everywhere,
All looking down, not up,
All looking at their phones.

The Holy Spirit said to me,
The phones will be more than that,
They are for buying, selling, everything,
That is the downfall of man.

Money will be obsolete,
Food will be phone bought,
Everything will go through the numbers,
This is a sign of the end.

Take note, take heed,
This is not to frighten or scare,
This vision is to warn of what is to come,
Jesus, our Lord is taking us home.

AMEN.
By The Holy Spirit using the hand of Melanie Woolner.

The dusty path

As I walked along the narrow, dusty path,
The white chalk hurt my feet,
All through the soft leather of my sandals,
The white dust arose like smoke about me.

As I walked along the narrow, dusty path,
I looked about me to see what could be,
Many prostrated, bowed figures in white,
Dotted all along as far as my eyes could see.

As I walked along the narrow, dusty path,
I saw grass verges at my left and right,
As I looked straight ahead,
A figure in dazzling white,
Arms outstretched,
Smiling, shining, beckoning me on.

As I walked along the narrow, dusty path,
The figure I saw was huge,
Getting bigger and bigger as I stepped closer,
He opened his arms, even wider,
He smiled even brighter,
As I approached, wanting to run,
As fast as I could, but able only to walk,
I couldn't get there fast enough,
To the prize, the goal, the crown.

As I walked along the narrow, dusty path,
I saw a crystal sea,
With rainbows all about in hues,
That my eye has never seen,
The enormity of it all was overwhelming,
Like a dream, a vision, a heart stopping moment,
But this was real, I felt the reality,

Not of this world, but the next,
I know where I'm going,
It's into the kingdom,
The kingdom of heaven,
To Jesus, My Jesus,
My prize, My goal,
My comfort, My crown,
My Love.

AMEN.
By The Holy Spirit using the hand of Melanie Woolner.

Treasure

What is treasure?
A prized possession, riches bounty?
We are treasure to God!
A treasure to hold, a treasure to have,
A possession more valuable than gold,
More valuable than jewels,
Even more than all the gems in the world,
Even more than all in the world.

We are God's treasure,
Beauty to behold,
A shiny, dazzling, perfect stone,
A wonder to behold,
More valuable than silver,
More valuable than any precious metal,
Even more than the entire world can hold.

We are children of God,
His prized possessions,
We are rich, we are glorified,
we are heirs to his kingdom,
Princes, princesses, our crowns are waiting,
Our rewards are great,
Our blessings are his love pouring out on us,
Falling down from heaven like gold coins from the purse of God,
Raining down on us,
As angels sing, all heaven rejoicing,
As we put up our hands,
Praise God and receive what he wants to give,
Which is everything we will ever need.

AMEN.
By The Holy Spirit using the hand of Melanie Woolner.

Oil and water

Like oil and water, heaven and earth cannot mix,
Like a magnet, I feel heaven's pull,
I feel a repelling of this world,
I feel a jarring, a pulling away from all things earthly,
I see, hear, feel differently and as a new creation I should,
But more than that, for I feel the sands of time are about to stop.

I feel a shift, a spiritual awareness that I haven't felt before,
It keeps getting stronger as I grow more mature,
This planet has nothing to offer me now,
I need to go home, I'm sure,
I need my heavenly body now,
I need to be free of this world.

I awake in the early hours,
Praying in tongues to the Lord,
I know time is short; He is coming back soon,
The angels are getting ready,
They are getting into position,
Jesus is calling us home.

AMEN.
By The Holy Spirit using the hand of Melanie Woolner.

On the way

As you go on your way,
Be as Jesus today,
Walk His walk,
Talk His talk,
Step into His sandals and do His works.

Whether you're shopping,
Working, cooking, cleaning,
Whatever you're doing,
Wherever you're going,
Walk with Jesus and do as He does.

Look for the supernatural,
Listen to Jesus' words,
Respond to Jesus' calling,
Do all that you've learned,
In the word.

Go where you are sent,
Pray for those who need it,
Heal those who are sick,
Visit those who are lonely,
Aid the afflicted and weak.

It's not enough to read only,
We must be doers as well,
We need to act when we're asked to,
We need to respond to His call,
We must be more than we are in the world.

We are more than flesh and blood,
We are more than skin and bone,
We are spiritual beings,
With a purpose in this world,
But not of it.

We are filled with the Holy Ghost,
We are born again,
We are on the side of angels,
We are church,
In every sense of the word.

We can move mountains,
We can bind up evil,
We can see into Heaven,
We can do anything,
We can do all in Christ.

We who have Christ in us,
We are all in all,
We have the power,
To do the impossible,
To change the world.

AMEN.
By The Holy Spirit using the hand of Melanie Woolner.

The flood within

God's river has started to flow,
From deep within me,
A spiritual flood gate has been breached,
A flood of the Holy Spirit has begun,
Flowing out into the natural,
From the supernatural within to the natural out.

The Holy Spirit has flooded my heart,
My body is not my own,
My spirit is filled, grown, swelled up,
My spirit is pumped up with the holy One,
My life is not my own, I belong to God.

The outpouring I feel is like a torrent, a storm,
A tempest from within.
This flowing of the spirit is urging me on,
Pushing, flowing, fast, like a swell, a surge of water,
Living water, a gigantic wave of spirit filled love.

God's waterfall, tidal wave, the spirit flowing is almost overwhelming,
Crashing down waves, like the sea is on fire,
A submerging of myself into the water of you,
Then holding me up, keeping me afloat, above the breakers and dangers.

You save me, rescue me, keep me from the deep,
You will not let go, you will not leave,
You are forever here, inside, just out of sight,
But not from my mind, not from my heart,
Not for even a moment.

AMEN.
By The Holy Spirit using the hand
of Melanie Woolner.

When I sing

When I sing, I sing to you,
O Saviour of my soul.
When I dance, I dance for you,
O Lord of Lords.
When I laugh, I laugh with you,
O King of Kings.
When I smile, I smile at you,
For you are here, are all things.

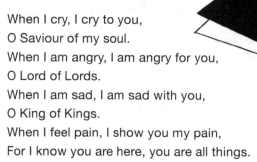

When I cry, I cry to you,
O Saviour of my soul.
When I am angry, I am angry for you,
O Lord of Lords.
When I am sad, I am sad with you,
O King of Kings.
When I feel pain, I show you my pain,
For I know you are here, you are all things.

When I pray, I pray to you,
O Saviour of my soul.
When I speak, I speak for you,
O Lord of Lords.
When I dream, I dream with you,
O King of Kings.
When I love, it is for you,
For I know you are here, you are all things.

AMEN.
By The Holy Spirit using the hand of Melanie Woolner.

You are the one

You are the one who,
You gave me life,
You gave me life,
You gave me life.

You are the one who,
I do adore,
You gave me life,
You gave me life.

You gave me life,
A life worth living,
You gave me all,
The things I need,
You gave me life,
You gave me life,
You gave me life,
You gave me life.

You gave me children,
When I asked you,
You gave them life,
You gave them life.

You gave me love,
When I needed that too,
You gave me life,
You gave me life.

You gave me life,
A life worth living,
You gave me all,
The things I need,
You gave me life,
You gave me life,
You gave me life,
You gave me life.

AMEN.
By The Holy Spirit using the hand of Melanie Woolner.

You clothe us

You clothe us with the sky,
You clothe us with the tabernacle of your church,
Your love surrounds us,
As space surrounds the earth,
Your love is never ending,
Never ceasing,
Never dwindling,
Your love for us is infinite,
As far as the east is from the west,
Never ending,
Never waning,
Never will anything surpass this love.

AMEN.
By The Holy Spirit using the hand of Melanie Woolner.

Your blood

Your blood pours down
Like sweet, sweet rain,
Clothing, reviving, again and again.

Your blood was shed
To cover our sins,
To soak us in love
And hide in your wings.

Your blood sustains us,
Strengthens, protects,
Nurtures, cleanses,
Covers and bedecks.

Your blood is your gift
To us, you're beloved,
Take it, use it, and accept it,
As the perfect present, ours to covet.

Your blood, Lord Jesus,
Is our armour of light,
Our garment of praise in the
Day and the night.

Your blood is love,
The heart and soul,
It makes us whole,
It makes us bold.

AMEN.
By The Holy Spirit using the hand of Melanie Woolner.

The sinners prayer

Dear God,

I believe Jesus died so that I can be forgiven.

I admit I have done wrong things and not lived my life how you want me to.

I'm sorry.

Please forgive me and come into my life to help me live your way.

From this moment on, I want to follow Jesus' example and join other Christians in Serving you and other people.

AMEN.

A special Thank you
Pastor George Macmullan of the Nazerine church for
much encouragement and prayers.

Also a BIG thank you to all who have read this book.
God Bless you